The Gymnast of Inertia

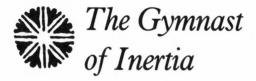

The Gymnast
of Inertia

Poems by William Hathaway

Louisiana State University Press
Baton Rouge and London   1982

Designer: Joanna Hill
Typeface: Plantin
Typesetter: G & S Typesetters, Inc.
Printer: Thomson-Shore, Inc.
Binder: John Dekker and Sons

Grateful acknowledgment is made to the editors of the following, in which several of these poems have appeared, sometimes in slightly different form: *Apple Street Anthology* (New Orleans Poetry Forum, 1977), *Chariton Review*, *Chiaroscuro*, *Columbia*, *Concerning Poetry*, *Discover*, *Graffito*, *Images*, *Interface*, *Mississippi Review*, *New Laurel Review*, *New Letters*, *New Orleans Review*, *North American Review*, *Northeast*, *Poetry NOW*, *Pontchartrain Review*, *South and West*, *Southern Review*, *Telescope*. "Time in the Woods" first appeared in the *Cimarron Review* and is reprinted here with the permission of the Board of Regents for Oklahoma State University, holders of the copyright. "Sunshine, LA" first appeared in *Three Rivers Poetry Journal*, copyright © 1981 by Three Rivers Press.

Library of Congress Cataloging in Publication Data

Hathaway, William, 1944–
  The gymnast of inertia.

  I. Title.
PS3558.A75G9   811'.54   81-18584
IBSN 0–8071–0981–9   AACR2
ISBN 0–8071–0982–7 (pbk).

For Baxter Hathaway
My thanks to Marie Blanchard for her help
with this manuscript

Contents

I

✵ *For the Soul of Karl Wallenda*

Kid Paret, knocked silly,
was caught in the ropes and Emile
Griffith killed him and we yelled
at the TV, the referee, but we
never yelled at Emile Griffith.
Now, that was wrong.

Oh, I have no right to blame
Karl Wallenda, or the wind,
or the cameraman with his grim
slowmotion, or my own wide, greedy eyes
and thrilling heart. But I do.
In truth, my senses waver before
the furious satyrs, rushing toward
some passionate barricade, who would
be buried with the wreckage of their bikes.

Empty-handed and guilty, some dull light
of afternoon forced through heavy drapes,
I stood over pancaked faces—"At peace at last."

"A man knows it must be so, and submits.
It will do him no good to whine,"
said Johnson, horrified by death,
to Boswell. I mean my whine to be
a pistol held against your breast to see
how you behave. Wallenda, you were scared,
I saw you clutching at the air.
My stomach clutched and I grew mad.
I was ashamed my children watched
you die, and shamed that they should see
me cry. It was a little cry from anger,
not grieving for our common fear.

Listen, I hate this stern truth:
there is no art in falling, the beauty
is to stay. Aloft, balancing the long
baton like pure justice, you were art.
Plummeting in the clear sun of San
Juan into black traffic you became
another star that streaked down out
of sight behind the curve of our vague hope.
Vain murderer of hope like Emile Griffith,
I'm half in love with your easeful sleep.

The Gymnast of Inertia
from Hart Crane

An Ancient man, more silenced than senile, is sent off on a plane

My blood leaps out to blue sky
at the window where a curtain blows.
The rumble of cars is joyous,
thrilling the nodding of tulips.
I am so excited! My heart drum-
rolls the bones while the loose meat
flows back for an ecstatic snap.

Such is memory. With bony arms
akimbo I take my ribs in my hands
and hunch like an antique teacup,
a windy cave where a paunch
once mooned. So, "this is my handle,
this is my spout . . ." Handled
like radium, like infectious death,
shouted tenderly into a blue sedan.

The motor hums a certain speed, colors
flicker an ascertained pace.
This world is aflame with fevers
from the sun. My steady ague
like a small wheel clicking against
larger cogs of a hurled clock
trembles. My cataracts match
a blur of newsprint pinned
and crumpled about a lamp-post.

My guts suck back, my lips
cannot unpeel their grin
and at attention I am carried aloft.
I would weave along the wing
and float down into soft, cotton clouds.
They are the dead, ghosts of my lovers

mingled as mist. They are the tears
that have gone to heaven to wait
the return of the dead, my lovers.
My lovers, mingled as dew to bathe
awake a new world drowsing
in the morning's first splendor.

Now down into sparkling lights
cushioned in the velvet night.
This body free of its own volition,
in its last innocence is one memory
descending to all memories at last.
All lights merge in a single radiance.
A bump, thunder of applause,
the long sigh and triumphant rush
as my eyes focus on the pulsing circle
dwindling back, away in the empty air.

If we forgot the The Faith of Our Fathers,
that plowing by moonlight,
it was not angry choice. Once we alone
argued like Hebrews in our clapboard temples.
We would love to believe
our righteous ancestor stalked past complacent
pews, hand in hand with an invisible angel,
but really we dozed off
in church. The wood-stove's waves of heat,
the sermon's torporous drone was too much
for us; we only dreamed
that walk among the ancient trees.

It was a silent dream, of course:
a hawk's shadow whose dark, undulant passage
froze the prairie dog stiff to the dull dun
of his mound, so only wind moaned
in the grasses. And it was wilderness,
our only cathedral, pulsing greener than
any green, in surge with our erotic terror.
White, radiant beams made holy places
in rich decay where we stood, moist
as new shoots, either deaf or totally alone.
And still, in our other eye the black shadow,
trembling like blowing silk, lapped up
the plains, silencing all it had darkened.

We believe our dreams travel
out over the many-colored cars in the lot,
up into rarer air above our city,
and there diffuse. Our own great sigh
will awake us to shake the hands that clasp us
as we step into Sunday light.
Always a shred of dream remains,
some somber ripple in our gray, wrinkled brains.

The orphans cut up in line
like other kids. Their keeper
is a college kid, no Fagin
who could make them mind
the value of these *objets d'art*
or teach their little hands
to seize this shiny moment
and return. These strong, loud
boys, girls in barbie dresses
can't be the waifs we yearned to be.
After all, birth *is* a crime! Life
is no museum picnic; our days
are spent weaving sunlight into money.
Even at night our eyes are on the hill,
glittering windows of the rich
so cold and bright, so unlike
the smoldering fever of our hope.

Still wild they throw baloney
at the fountain's mouth. My own
peanut butter days come back,
before my blood turned cunning
with desire and only raced amuck
for fun. Their innocence is too dull.
My heart and hand tense with need
to correct their ways. Not yet on my own,
but truly orphans I must walk
away down rows of pictures to the door.
It is not my job to love these well-fed
foster children of the state.
Their way is paid as my keep
is earned in a clean light of industry.
Only once in the first chug
of their chartered bus can I smell
that buried fear, that ancient misery.

Side by side we sit in the dark Bauhaus
surrounded by signs that flash and gurgle.
I am drinking a Sturm und Drang, pineapple
garnish sculpted as "The Rape of the Sabine
Women." Your drink is called Lachrymose.
Now and then a black shape slides off
a stool and stumbles toward the smell
of urine. Here and there a sudden face flares
up, chiaroscuro studies of solitude perhaps
lit by "raging furnaces in the heart."
False night falls again, laced with sulphur.
Tranquilly our wet fingers contemplate
the table's initials. Deep within I compose
a sigh and in the darkness hear your answer.

Across the street lightning hits a barbecue pit
splattering Bakersfield with tiny bits of hamburger.
Collars up, heads bowed, we start into the gale
for a tramp in the country. A small dog licks
meat off a bank window. From a gas station
a radio sings in the real language of workers.
It is a song about a one-night stand in a Chevy van.
I reach over and take your chilly, white hand
in mine because we are so young and unhappy.
Let's die very young and never, never be boring!
Tonight by firelight, we will leaf through *The Joy
of Sex* and weep, trembling in exquisite misery.

Poe

PAS DE CHANCE!
Poor Baudelaire thought Poe unlucky
and drunk. And probably worse.
All who care swirl away,
sweep up in his vicious beauty,
because hidden behind
a slimy organ a green elf
squats in all of us.

Oh, Edgar Allan Poe
I can waltz, polka and weave
alone to your steady tunes.
Your great prose stings my eyes
like smoke from a childish campfire.
I will never forget you,
who knew and hated evil.

Poe called liquor "ashes" and changed
language forever. He loved his child
wife who bled to death hungering.
They call sadness depression now,
anger with yourself. He knew guilt
and sadness. Brave and elegant words
were a halo around this difficult man.
We still dream before sleep
of eating breakfast with Poe.
Our frayed black suits
mirrored in the cantaloupe pool.

I want to read the meters of Edgar
Poe and remember that cool sand
bathing my feet when I danced
alone and was free, completely free,
by the starstruck sea.

Through its many lenses the fly can see
dogs which hear for miles, goats digesting
impossible cans, perhaps a truculent alligator
clocking forty-five miles per hour on flat
ground to the poacher who curses and prays
to the slick trunk of the cypress.

Our great gift is language, but that is not
our salvation. If ever you dream we're God-
like hang around the dimestores; no link
is really missing. Generations of carefree
incest, hunger and syphilis rummage six-
fingered there; so goblined by brute time
the bright crime-spying mirrors distort them
back to beauty, of a sort. Too swarthy for
those fluorescent aisles, they should roost
in trees, beasts of the woods snarling at their
soles, and them growling back in the language
of wind and rocks with tongues the color of dirt.

Our tongues are pink. We packed our mouths
with words like pebbles and spoke against the sea.
Surrendering pebbles to the gloomy well we can-
not guarantee a splash. This needs no proof.
That is why we kiss: such sweet, saliva balm
of your tongue soothing mine, a soft poultice
for that tenderness from the grinding scrape of words.

Yes, touch is your answer, but in stale, victorian
halls professors bump heads again, chasing birds
in the dark. Lost in thought in full daylight
they bicycle into parked cars. "Eureka, a referent!
Let us whimsically call it Pain." Mistaking
the creaking of dry boards for song our al-
chemists conclude no rhythm to the spheres.

You and I with a "higher kind of play" have found
better uses for the spaces between the words.

Deep beneath the flotsam and jetsam of vast seas
whales moan and bleat: great groaning prayers
straight from great hearts. Forlorn, forlorn
our own lungs heave. Do we curse or pray?
Who listens? Ah yes, on that it all depends.
Et tout le reste est en abyme.

❋ *The Model's Lecture*

You will note my head is a diamond;
do not ignore the hint of savagery in my
high cheekbones and broken nose. My round
paunch conceals the hungering years so draw me
thinner there than I appear. Nor can you greatly
err in adding authority to the chin or by
straightening a shoulder where decades of woes
have curved it out of dignity. Surely you intend
more than a mute depiction of this superficial frame,
this spare, awkward spirit-cage. Listen! Beyond
the scratch and rub of charcoal, the dull hum
of air-conditioning in the vaulted studio, you can
hear a rising murmur of ancient song. It comes from
here, in here where a wild yet weary sea crashes
on the shingles of an English coast. O if you could
reproduce the blue of my eyes you could paint
that sough of lonely wind that bends the grasses
fringing cliff and dune. And lick your lips;
yes it is salt. Gulls are screaming, screaming
in taut, white fury out where waves rinse black rocks.
Breaking the painful, unnatural pose I stalk
among your easels and what do I see but you,
always you, reflected in my diamond shape.
Where is the shy child, the nervous lover, self-
righteous drunk, your loyal friend hiding?
Oh yes, I see him with you now. There
he comes along the strand waving his arms
and singing, louder and louder he is waving
and singing as the wind tears the song from his mouth.

Toads fill the day with raucous cries of love
and at night get down to business. *Amplexus:*
a fierce grip belly on back until seed and eggs
spill everywhere and the toad on top relaxes.

In a dark time an Italian priest tortured
toads once while they mated to determine
the depth of toadlike passion. He learned
their will was stubborn, if not their ardor.

Despite the grim tenacity of some, not all toads
embrace. Others masturbate and then bounce
against each other in a mad afterthought of dance
and still no strange clergy can divine the reason.

Do toads lust, or does some secret clock spasm
their indifferent will to imitate our godlike vices?
It seems the humble facts unlock a question.
I'll say pure love is making in the garden,

if only for an instant, and the shrieks we hear
are songs in celebration of manifest creation.
One from some hundreds will leave water for
our brilliant air and I choose to think the toads

with a higher kind of knowing really care.

Breakfast is cognac, a cozy fire
for the stomach, to numb the lips
and let swamp trees grow emerald
in the morning mist. We fish
for crappie, imagine their huge eyes
aglow in a cold tangle of roots.
Before day, before history the wood
is swollen black, the water murky
with danger, all beasts eternally pregnant,
grunting in labor. We are drunk.
A reptile becoming a bird groans
in the trees. A purple tongue hangs
from the fish's mouth and its bright
blood drips to beetles in palmetto.
Our eyes turn old and terribly keen;
hair grows in our shoes; a stink
of dinosaur, flies clouding their mouths
and eyes. But light comes, we break
out the beer. The fish begin to bite.
Great bubbles surface and softly belch
around us. Ancient gases of the dead?
No. Frogs are farting in their sleep.

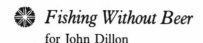 *Fishing Without Beer*

for John Dillon

The bait assumes new urgency at daybreak.
We feared sharp outlines and responsible intent
would exasperate us into tense, dull silence,
but a natural mist hovers the pond, blurs
stately spaces in the trees. A pair of yellow
flickers take air together in loose harmony
of flight, high and low in the openness the pond
provides. Once, as sunlight wobbled onto field
and copse, we might have thought them maenads
come to signal the opening of daytime
fishing rites. Today we are glad they
are just private birds engaged in a mundane
discipline of catching bugs for breakfast.

We trust the farmer who owns this pond
will also keep his place; we will not start
at every groan and whistle from the shadowy
bank. Even our bateau behaves with humility;
instead of a motor's assertive roar and sudden
blast of fake wind we watch small whirlpools
from the paddle gyre back gracefully in our wake.
And the fishing itself is no orgiastic struggle
of pole against bass, with wild whoops and boat-
rocking lurches. Delicately we cast our flies to
bright spots of sun warming in the richer shade
of toppled limbs. The bream catch is steady
and only an occasional splash from our swelling
stringer surprises the calm of this peaceful work.

You know, the stink of beer and fish together
aroused erotic yearnings in us once, so
humid air thickened with violence and I am sure
our voices went coarse and shrill over still water.
Do we regret those meaty days of anxious manhood

under "the meat-eating sun"? No, our blood sings
yet to a full moon and at dawn our fingers can
surely unravel holy madness into a thing of beauty.

The Poet Hunts Doves
with the Natchitoches Police
for Jim Dyson

A man's handle is Polar Bear and he
asks for Roughneck's ten-twenty.
It is seven thirty, hungover
and crushed in the cab of a pick-up.
So many fantastic dials and gauges!
Jimmy calls himself Pervert over
the thick highway air to Roughneck.
If asked to speak I would be
Captain Video—"Video" for short.

We ease down into the soft brown field,
awhir with hidden creatures, load up
shotguns and squat in high weeds to wait.
Doves sail over alone, in pairs, in threes,
like fighter planes lost from formation.
Sharp reports, puffs of feathers, a bit-
ter rain of pellets and often everywhere
that high halloo "Doves, boys, doves!"
My own hands darken with blood.

I never knew how easy it is to shoot,
and hit. I try to think of Turgenev
but only *Field & Stream* in a dentist's
office will surface. The wounded bird
hops ahead as I try to gun-butt it dead.
"Hey New York, this ain't no golf course."
The voice of God from out of the brush.

There in the truck's bed mounds of gray
dead, beyond the limits of law or sense.
Sour whiskey finally at peace in my belly,
accepted as friend, finally, when all is said
and done. The smell is nothing and we
save the tiny red hearts with the fleshy

breasts to eat. More whiskey to burn
out the feather tickling in the throat,
to ease the violence of the night, to
celebrate the loneliness of being men.

✳ *The Stuttering Parachutist*

Wah-Wah-Wah-ONE!
Tuh-Tuh-Tuh-TWO!
Th-Th-Th-THREE!
The ground leapt up
slamming him into blackness.

Many times we've waited on a chair edge
for the end of a word to explode.
Wives of stutterers live in silence,
or drenched in spittle they bite
their own tongues swollen with
unfinished sentences. Children
of stutterers suffer an eternity
of wisdom, a slow machine-gunning
of rage or praise. They must swallow
air with involuntary sympathy.

We can only imagine what dark vision
charged the first pause, sprung the coil
of the tongue so it fluttered loose
in a windless mouth. Affliction
of fear and hatred. How the face
twists in effort to form those outrageous
words! Guilt of the onanist's hand
struck to the mouth in terrible irony.
What dread compassion we feel,
amazed by the smooth trip of
our speech as if there were no complicity.
Surely we will stutter in hell.

But the stuttering parachutist will
not wait. We are the prattling, mindless
finches, all melody and no substance.
He croaks the numbers with loud disdain
and look, the cord is flying free.

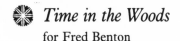 *Time in the Woods*
for Fred Benton

We all know people who easily think like fish;
"If I was a blue-gill I would love this cool hole,
shaded by oak, freshened by this clean runlet
from a woodland spring." We look up to the tangle
of line, hooks, bobbers and flies webbing the limb
and our errant minds absently total the investment
in that tree. It is certain we will disturb few fish.

We come because the woods and water give our loneliness
more dignity than all the brittle smiles in town.
The history of this land, this property, makes more sense
than the circumstance we call our lives. Beneath mounds
and grassy settles are bones and bits of metal from
a conflict so old and finalized their pure study calms
a mind churned by feelings. Was this clump of rust
a rifle's guts, or a cache of buttons fused back to earth?
Was this some yankee's arm, or merely looted dinner?

Washing sand free in the same ageless stream
that polished the stone, we can hold eons comfortably still
in our palms. Art without artists—the blessed fossil
offers sweet intricacy, hallowed age without jabber.
They click in coat pockets like money we would feed
to no machine. Shell in hand, bird on the wing,
the sun's fire ablaze in water, great trees strong
against the sky like patient fathers. Why do our lives
lack this simple grace? We are pierced by yearning,
transfixed in the only moment we have, will ever have.

There, where we are always in, where all we fling
away flies back again, we only need the wind
across our brows. Wind no photograph can show,
which blows away those latin names we stapled
to the twigs, now nesting with that fishing snarl
in trees and milky pools until all letters pale.

Not just dust but also gases,
Liquids, all in flux: the only stasis.
And as the wretched ancients said
"When you're earth you're dead."

But when you're quick you're hot
So hi-ho, let's drink to this earth
Which is us, saved by a virgin birth,
And sing and sport and screw around a lot.

For misery leads us through dark alleys
And we shall not want the funeral lilies
When earth dumps on earth before
Solemn suits quacking "evermore."

Waking then from that sweet sleep
To blink forever in other-earthly light,
Always banished from mysterious night,
We'll know our furious pride comes cheap.

So earth rages earth down below
But we clutch all earth, afraid to go.
Without regrets for youth I would not dwell
Homesick in heaven or unashamed in hell.

✿ *Incoming Squall at Twilight*

First, thinking only evening comes, I see
the seabirds streaming in from the sea's far rim,
and hear their high gibber quaver plaintively
muffled to my ears and I could envy them
their clear sky and song. But then like a new land
colored cold indigo against the shimmery blue
a storm bulges that horizon, fast rising so it stands
like a purple backdrop to the empty, gleaming view.

How thin shadows sprawl when a sudden silence falls
before the inland scamper. At my feet I see the first
twinkling sand tumble over, then loosened sail
off to knock a million free. The thin grasses twist
to snarls and the sea oats' tassels tug toward
serene, dark hollows of dunes and distant lights.

At the edge of dune and beach I watch the forward
trudge of my small loved ones; her robe once white
now glows electric blue and the littlest waddles blind
behind a striped beachball as if it is the whole
world she must save. Then, as if this wild wind
scrapes my heart with sand, once again I feel
a fierce and ancient ache, a yearning loneliness.

So crying words they cannot hear above the blast
and rumble of blackened beach I press
back to them, again frantic for their outstretched grasp.

✺ Dentistry

I close my eyes and watch a trillion suns,
now dead, still guided by living ones;
memory offspring of his great lamp's glare
squirming miserably in my welling tears.

In and out the needle—a bitter taste
like spoiled plums, dark blood is traced
in the flushing bowl and the tongue turns
to a wedge of cheese and ceases to discern

its proper place in speech or touch.
Under the descending whine I flinch
to frightened meat like a sober virgin
or wounded deer. Eyes squeezed shut again

(one must submit) I feel that magic nerve
catch fire and flame as his cruel drill swerves
the rounds of my rottenness. I smell smoke
of funeral pyre, kitchen odor of a cannibal cook,

and my dead, swampy mouth flows over,
despite his feeble pumps, with bile and tooth slivers.
Oh precious is this agony, this testing of the will,
for the sermon of his drill must surely keep me out of hell.

All trials must end, even stars seek their way
in light and my tingling tongue can assay
proud, new gold instead of decaying coal.
Let the tongue of a golden girl mine this glory hole.

❋ *The Egrets*

No words can tell their stillness
as they fill the cypress tree,
so large, pure white against the light.
They don't know our water's sick,
our fish are poison. They see
the sun flash forth in the glory of day
and lift off to feed in majestic curves.

Even alive it looks stuffed for science
or schoolchildren on the turtle-littered
log, which empties as we pedal by.
Everything knows that we eat everything.
We see egrets through a haze of heat
or tears. Our eyes build the case
and painted scene; all blackens but
this square which hums its fluorescent
beams into the hidden jello of our eyes.

And if egrets could talk to men
it would be in French, from a long way
off, boring as the weather news.
A stubby, muscular tongue heaves
fish back into the sleek neck,
the neck that snaps the dagger beak
deep into the warm pool. Oh,
to have such equipment! We would
suffer the beady eyes that only know
the movement of food or fear.
In twilight or morning mist we
would ghost down to the island
of silence and alone glow like the north.

✺ *Tousle*

An emerald creeps across
my brussels sprouts. My rump
is solid, taking root in fresh
soil—sweet odor of worms and rot.
I'm proud of my little gem. Each
leg has three tiny hooks that catch
fiber, up or down it is a tentative
climb. Green on green. We feast
together on the sun's radiance.
Your cool shadow changes all

colors. Your cool fingers, snake-
dry and smooth, tousle my hair
and I'm deep in that crystal
bubble that sprouts a virgin's tear
at a twig joint. I'm where blind
whales sleep and snort, dream-
ing in black, subterranean sea.
When I stand for your embrace
one hundred suns race to greet
us. Our eyes, moist as snails, close
and our tongues worm for salt
in the first pulsing caves.

✳ *Pain Perdu*

Clean and dripping we step out
of sublime, porcelain cells, where we sang
the morning prayer of ourselves,
into the fragrance of bacon and french toast,
that *pain perdu* with its secret spice of vanilla.

Through the long night our sins skipped
freely in unguided dreams, but daybreak
brings hunger and with that some humility.
Like a relic of last night's love this odor
and taste remain to feed our immortality.

See how morning sun hits the crystal vase!
HAZAK HAZAK VINITHAZAK*
In one blinding moment we are cleansed and fed.

*Be strong, Be strong, And let us strengthen one another.
(Hebrew scriptural refrain)

The dullest people I knew
gathered round my bed,
the ones who made me feel
stupid or ashamed when I
was living. My flustered
wife held my hand like a fish,
worried our children might
eat poorly at the neighbor lady's.
Outside the door I heard
the nurse with massive arms
send off students who learned
nothing from me, but came
anyway for final grade changes.
And while my mother's clergy-
man read aloud the governor's
telegram I died. What did
I care, bobbing off in dark
blue sea, under light blue sky?

I liked your poems "Michael," "We Are Seven,"
and "Idiot Boy" very much, even when
the teacher read them aloud and cried
and blew her nose. "Tintern Abbey" is really neat,
though I don't understand it. I did a walk-
athon for March of Dimes once. I hate your poem
"Daffodils." Ha-ha, that's just a joke,
I just don't know better because of television.
Seriously, why did you become such a crusty,
old poo-poo? Professor Borck at the university
says you got tired of not being rich. My
dad says poor people are happy being poor
because God loves everyone—even poets. I
think it would be romantic to have a French
girlfriend and a dopefiend for a best friend.
I can hardly wait until my creepy sister
goes to college and I can have her room.
My best friend is Veralee Broussard and I can
talk about anything with her. I wish you
could tell me what it's like to be dead.
It would feel neat to lie in a cozy coffin
underneath the flowers and know everything.
Really, you rot and go to heaven or hell.
Well, this is almost two hundred words, so
I have to go. Tomorrow we read Amy Lowell.
Mrs. Curtis says she smoked cigars!

✳ *The Initiation*

First we'd let the New Boy into the shed,
our clubhouse, dark and smelly with mystery.
Then in hard, hushed voices we'd intone
our Secrets and our Mission. Then we'd
tell him what he had to do and if he didn't
he must die, horribly. We told him about
the Boy who didn't, who squealed to his dad,
the cops, and how he died. Ask anyone.
Then we let him shake and fart alone in the shed
while we passed a Camel in the sunlight.
So down at the sooty dump his cheeks
quivered like gray jello when we tied
his hands to the tree and tears burst out
when we tore his new shirt right up the back.
As the iron glowed cherry-white in the coals
the Boy wept and pleaded and babbled
his crazy promises and threats. Be a
Man we said, Buck up, and stoked
the fire and tenderly turned the rod
in its raging nest. How he wrestled when
we tied the blindfold on! His body stiff
as a dry pine board. And when the hidden
ice was jammed against his back
his scream was animal and pure as
Love. We held his limp body like a lamb
and bathed his lips with ice till he came back.
That's how we did it, then.

William Hathaway, 1878–1958

"Renounce the faithlessness of thy parents and bathe
in the Blood of the Lamb," he once wrote to me.
My father, furious and hurt, paced the room
with an old grudge frozen bright in the eye
he cast on me. I did not flinch, but wondered.

I still wonder what was my namesake's shame?
Hathaway means "lives way out on the heath"
I'm told and hushed rumor says a spice
of "eccentricity" lurks in the chromosomal stew.
You could have fooled me. The nice normality

of this crew, except for him, would send
a flower club off to profound and dreamless sleep.
"How can a family reproduce for over three hundred
years in this golden land and not produce
a single notable?" my father once complained.

I'll tell you, we never liked the heath,
always wanted to move to town and join clubs.
Old William was a poor farmer, who yearned
for souls to save in town, and most of Michigan.
His was the peculiar learning of the self-taught

and he spoke out like Jeremiah in Kalamazoo.
Hell, you've got to love people to tell them
off like that, and there the puzzle begins to fit.
The gospel was his way to the hearts of men,
since he had no money, influence, or degree.

My path was strong drink and godless art,
but the vision stays the same. Lord, how
I'd like to bust up a temple and send those
moneychangers squealing after scattered coins.
Awake! Awake! We are home from the wilderness,

wild-eyed and bushytailed. Tremble before
our righteousness and obey. Above all, love
us, for we fear the coming night and the fire
next time. Sweet Mercy, meet me in the garden
when the dew is on the rose. Heal me, Father, heal me.

Wisdom Crieth Without: She Uttereth Her Voice in the Streets

for Herbert Rothschild

Listen! Our friend Wisdom is drunk again.
Thrown from the saloon she staggers the streets
and concourses of mid-day whining at shoppers
and secretaries coming back from lunch.
Yanking at her disheveled frock, her make-up
streaked with tears and sweat, eyes crazed
red with grief and breath stinking, who
would believe she was the Darling of our class?
She has lost her purse, but it isn't drinking
money she wants, or even a ride to the suburbs.
Youth ends in age, she says, and the busy
life is blind. What have you done with all my
pretty ones? she asks. Why do you recoil
from my reproof? They walk firmly in the face
of her wail, for indeed, to listen is to begin
response. Her demand is no less than human
love. They would not promise what they would
not give. If this persists the police will come
to all our shame. Herb, this is pitiful.
We must go in your car to the heart of our
town and bring her babbling back to Knowledge,
her husband, and her children, Courage and Faith.
Yes, the devices he bought her sit cold
in the kitchen and her family sups on fruit
of their own purchase. They would divorce her
for her errant ways, but it is not our place
to blame. Good neighbors, we mask our anger,
murmur words of hope and do our good deed grimly.

I thought you'd think
you were Napoleon, scratching
the imaginary itch, one eye
up the chimney while the other,
soft and reasonable, hid chaos
beneath a scheming lid.
And this is not so wrong.
Atremble with thorazine,
fingers swimming in your hair
you talk the future, as if
it's just a city, waiting job.
The place is all wrong.
Any moment you'll unslump,
arise to dance without music;
and trapped in your stiff, clumsy
arms I'll have to stumble
to your tune. Is our time
half over or half yet to go?
We are in the middle of morning
when outside rain ceases,
that moment before birds begin to sing.
I feel your heart swell against
my chest. Broken, but working.

✤ *Apology for E. H.*

Oh, most natural grandson I was
to keep old skin at arm's length;
Stale breath in a polka-dot dress,
propped from car to chair on my strength.

It seemed you lived forever then, an Easter
fixture at the table's end, too old to chew
the ham, isolated, deaf and always bitter
that each year light dimmed and children grew.

From love and pain in your silent, blurry world
you jumped the gun with crisp hundred dollar bills,
searching each strange face for gratitude. We failed
you to the end, afraid of your fear, old woman smells.

Closer now, not from loss or virtue seen too late,
you swell my emptiness, materialize my fate.

✳ *Crawfishing*

That is a colorful regionalism for procrastination.
"Weaseling out" you might say in Michigan.
Who knows or cares? Here it has purpose.
Crawfishers throw nets, beef melt, pails, tow-
sacks and beer—yes, lots of half-cooled beer—
in a pick-up and *ils sont partis* for swampy
ditches off state highways. They lift the nets
with poles, because sometimes a cottonmouth
whips outraged off the bait, making adrenalin
sing with alcohol in the blood. But usually
one crawfish will make his stand, reared back
with one claw firmly in the string, the other
cocked against the gods. They guard their holes
thus. "Mudbugs" Cajuns call them, and it fits.
They swim forwards and backwards with spasmodic
convulsions of their tails in insect terror.
That is how crawfish crawfish.

Closer to the angels, my friends and I derived
more spiritual substance from the act.
Soaked with swamp-slime, streaked
with elemental mud we settled to the bank
and in growing fondness slowly drank beer,
sour with the fecundity of the swamp itself.
All the amazing greens mingled in a meaning
we could not find in town as we mellowed
beyond the need for words. Indeed, words were
said which in their feeling, more than sound
or wisdom, were like music that drifted up
shafts of light between the cypress trees.
Now I no longer drink beer and my warm friends
no longer take me to the swamp. No lament,
or even puzzlement; it was just a season's pastime.
And that, all of that, is crawfishing too.

On the top step with soft kitchen light
behind us and dank cellar glooming below
we sat together kneading the yellow into
white margarine. Older and stronger, you
always got the longest turn, I remember.
Mother's radio was always playing "Tunes"
by Percy Faith and his orchestra, I think.
That was the music we beat and squeezed to,
and it seemed the yellow product tasted better.

I lack patience with the college girl who cuddles
her new kitten in my class. She lets it crawl
underneath her sweater, between her terrific
breasts, and because I am weak I force a sickly
smile. This is not innocence, but its cynical
use. I would be labeled cynic if I leveled
a reproof, since the girls pretend to think
the cat is cute and the boys are dazzled by her tits.
Could I work this vignette into the text-
book honesty of Cordelia and Kent? Instead
I take a tangent with aimless anecdotes
of sibling rivalry. This kitten, class, and play
do not interest me as much as a memory of you
sliding back in focus—clutching our cat
in such sweet dishonesty when I came to punch
you back. O you knew my frail honor
would permit me to pound a girl, if she was
sister, but parental rules forbad
the striking of that cat. Other things come

back: the time you were spanked too for not
telling that I alone ruined Grandmother's fox
with gum. Later, shut together in the scary closet
with that dripping beast, its glass eyes
strangely lit with malice and reproach, we

were as close as we ever were. Your senseless
sacrifice made sense to you, I am sure. Though
it was not for my gratitude, I am grateful now.
I did not understand your female moods,
grown-up talk at table, or the love mush
on the radio. I still don't. Let me confess,
in Lear the only character I fully understand
is Edmund. Listen, do you remember what
I'm remembering now: *When-e-ver we kiss*
I wor-ry and won-der / you're close to me
now / but whe-re is your he-art?

The Souls of Dolphins

We do not know what souls are,
but after many days of sitting by the window
watching animals we believe they have them.
Cats and dogs have domestic, lazy souls.
Birds have nervous, greedy souls except
chickens and turkeys which have stupid souls.
Observe the busy ant, industrious honeybee;
they are loaded with communal soul.
Just show me a creature and I'll show you a soul.
Of course trees do not have souls,
but they serve as an inspiration to us all.
The greatest soul of all is the dolphin's. Why,
you ask? Because they have big brains and don't
bite us. Millions of years ago they returned
by starlight to the sea where their grasping,
egotistical fingers melted away and their eyes
grew wonderfully gentle. So are they blessed
even above the Jews, who were only chosen.

And Their Liberation

In California, where animals have more and purer
souls than anywhere else, two lab assistants
freed a scientist's dolphins to the midnight sea.
"Gone surfin" they wrote on the pool blackboard,
and signed the dolphins' slave names. Do we
applaud this altruism, since sharks (who
have the souls of sociopaths) quickly ate those
emancipated yet greenhorn dolphins? Ah yes
indeed, it follows that if worldly knowledge
leads not to salvation, ignorance must.
Like the moon-pulled surf itself those boys
were guided by "a knowledge of the heart—
natural savvy" (never call corn "corn," say maize

instead) as opposed to cold, soul-less science.
Like all good martyrs they are doing time for all
our souls. Listen to the soulful strains of their
mouthharps float through iron bars at twilight.
They "sing in their chains like the sea."

✳ *Baseball*

In baseball the great dramatic need we share
is to get back home again. I say this wist-
fully. Watch the drunks watch football at the bar.
That game is war, complete with armor, contest-
ed ground, and ranks of specialists. The ball
is slammed into defiled grass while the runner
prances his Hitler jig and home-front generals thrill
to unformed lusts for rape and pillage. But consider
the fastball pitch, so clean, so true; the crack
of the bat, so confident and proud. Legs churn
in yearning symmetry, the snapped ball streaks
back like a loathed star of fate which must return.
The girl in the stands serenely knits and unravels
her domestic yarn, oblivious to dust and indecorous catcalls.

✳ Nate's Dimple

Yes, quite a picture for the *Post*,
three bare-kneed boys lined on a horse's back.
But the horse, in no mood for kitsch, bolted
for the shade of his sulking pace, under the piers
of the great southern house. And the boys ducked,
except Nate, the goofy one who would always see
all things, so he sat flat in the bare dirt with
the horse's tail flicking his amazed, bleeding face.
No sense was knocked into his mellow brain,
nothing jarred loose, but forever in his smile
you will see God's touch given to those who ride
tall in the saddle, haloed by stars of innocence.

I   Once the millionaire's son, Vanderbilt,
owned these mountains, nationalized now
"for the enjoyment of the public."
Where once we poached we now pay
to file past imported treasures
aimlessly arranged by the National Park
Service. George "preferred the arts"
and "had little taste for finance."
We have brought nothing here ourselves,
except our raw, dumpy peasant bodies.
The colors of our vacation clothes
glow in the varnished paneling of another
age. We all imagine living here.
A cool drink perhaps on the high veranda,
Chopin floating out from the dark room
of Belgian tapestries. Hand on a child's
head we want to say before the view,
"Our mountains and lakes filled with
Our deer and fish. Our Whistler
on the wall and Our set of Zola
in red morocco." But by owning all
of it we are poor. This sad man's
bad taste cannot be replaced
to suit our notions of order in the hills.

II   Not like freed serfs gawking at the loot
of czars do we come to Cone Mansion.
Like any white farmhouse on a knoll
this house is free to enter—to buy
"mountain crafts" made by college kids.
Yes, we understand this man Cone
who built his house for scenery with
no thought of Blois or Azay-le-Rideau.
His pantyhose factory is in the valley
and we know his need to get away.

Rhododendron flowers under beech
trees that line paths tourists ride
their rented horses on. Bass below
in the mountain lake are free for any
licensed citizen to take. His gift
was clearly prompted by his taxes,
and haven't we too paid our tithes?
No matter the dulcimer we buy
won't play. The hippie who made
it was polite and our grass-stained
children fall asleep, too tired to fight.

III   My friends gone home, family all asleep
I take the scotch bottle and walk up
the mountain where the road turns
into path. The air, the stars, small
brook with bright stones are all cold.
The scotch tastes terrific and I fill
up with hopeful dreams. A long
and graceful future, love given
and returned seems possible now.
I see the ski-lift businessmen
from Florida built snaking up
between the pines. It's all bankrupt
now; condominiums, indoor tennis
courts and pools, all bad business
overextended and left to rust and rot.
Truly cold now I turn back, hooting
drunkenly back to the owls, who like me
own themselves and have no worries.

Sunshine, LA: A Pastoral

From the sleek interstate you can descend
into Sunshine like an equatorial tourist
swerving in disgust from an Ibadan "go-slow"
onto dusty African plains. So suddenly
vision is reduced to myriad shades of green
or brown, no others except the Dynamite
Lounge—so red and rectangular like a real
powder box you expect it to burst in furious,
roiling orange. Because the very air is humid
with chemical stench, greasy smoke of blow-outs,
and hatred. Rage so inert you cannot tell
if those jaundiced eyes live or see; indifferent
to glistening flies and passing whites who will
wisely never stop. Time stopped here. It makes
no difference if and when the washtub falls
from the rusty nail, or the ramshackle wall itself
makes a final creak and tumbles to the weeds.

Oh yes, the irony is obvious: a hamlet named
for a cowboy-governor's horse, a snatch of song,
a bridge built by graft which no one drives
because it spans nowhere to just another side.
Or is it all the other way around? Who cares?

The sun almost always shines in Sunshine,
relentlessly, and the hidden souls of these poor folk
run free in the streets in brilliant rooster bodies.
Raised to mate and fight, both birds and dogs
must live taut fury, or live to slink in a world
of kicks. Look into the eyes of those square, tailless
hounds, fur coarse as used Brillo pads, eyes that
bulge crimson with hate from the choking chains,
as you would look into a volcano where bad gods
live. But, friend, I would prefer you drove right

through to the famous river, to that gracious
"ante-bellum home" you wish to pay to see.
Listen to the summer thunder, always ominous
and imminent, and like guilt, always a promise
left to thirst. You do not deserve this pain.
God damn it, press that pedal to the levee
and race your engine at that pointless light.

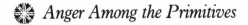

I   Landlocked, imprisoned far
from the dull violence of the sea,
left only with the rhythmic lapping
of words which seem to struggle
out of rock for harmony, not for sense
but a better efficiency, I rise at morning
like the Jivaro to drink tobacco juice,
vomit evil into weeds and recite
my hatreds to my sons. Rain pounds
on the roof while we sit in the smoky hut
drinking beer from the pot, planning mischief.
Only the strongest survive the rites of manhood,
so few bother. Anger begins with a certain gesture.
Rage shrieks from our dreams, a bird from the cliff,
tongue stiff in the open beak, talons aflame and flaring.

II   We've been drinking all night in different bars.
"In my country I am a king. Here a nigger!"
His red eyes hate me, the only one who will look
in this midnight diner his bitter whine is filling.
Probably we'll both be beaten up before dawn breaks.
He thinks I'll play the pimp to set things straight,
but he'll have to quench his own savage fires.
We've been drinking all night—me to forget,
him to remember, and both our countries still young.

III   "Everything I see is against my religion"
said the composer who went deaf, perhaps mad.
Off go the Little Stunted Lapps in uncomfortable
city suits to study themselves at the university.
How to castrate the lead deer with your teeth.
To learn the three thousand words for deer
and remake forgotten songs that made eyes gleam
around a fire. To become Lutheran ministers
and die of syphilis in the free hospitals of Sweden.

From the air they are a moving brown mass
speckled with red dots on the infinite field
of white—an organic flag denying its own state.
Like a Cheyenne dog, not something to love, but to eat.

IV   Angry with his boobish townsfolk Thoreau
said he pitied the state of Massachusetts,
and that jail was proper for the moral citizen.
And tonight on the evening news a black rapist,
face thick with fear and ignorance, said the same thing.
Hairy Ainu, Stunted Lapp, Headhunting Jivaro,
are these our primitives or the alliterative litany
of our ferocious dreams? I close my eyes and live
one thousand years trapped on the sun-blazed mesa.
The skinny corn withers and casts its bleak shadow.
My woman stumbles from the cool darkness of the French
priest's house. The earth sucks up her tears
and on the horizon is the continual glint of armor.
Sometime soon this mad flood rushing in my ears
will burst, these arroyos will groan with blood.
Mine or yours, I couldn't care less.

Out in the street women band
together to deny us sex. We
cower in doorways muttering
"What's up? What's up?"
That's what the smallest and oldest
of us asks from a distance,
his snotty hankie quavering on a golf
stick. They say, "Quit fighting
Sparta." We say, "O.K. come on home."
A good home-cooked meal, stewed
chicken, our favorite, and then a romp
in bed. Everything is terrific.
The babies squall on the stoop
with poopy pants while we horse
around in the dark, eat peeled grapes,
watch TV and don't fix up the house.
But it gets boring, you know,
so one by one we drift back
bye and bye to the Legion bar.
Pretty soon the phone's jangling
off the hook about cold dinner,
missing money, the children's car wrecks.
All of a sudden we're old and fat
and bald in the mirror alone
next to the jar for muscular dystrophy.
Vida Blue pitches a no-hitter
and everyone stands up hoping
behind the fence. Let 'em try
that number once again—just
try it! Too old to diddle around
under porchlights and walk home
top-heavy, the moon burns a hole
in our pockets and the car always starts.

I knew a man who like us awoke alone
in the midst of his life, in a dark wood.
Always in his home there was wet stillness
of impending storm and a moist, rich smell
of fear wafted from the shadows of open doors.
His verse never advertised sick spirit like
my mean complaints I called "laments."
His wife was beautiful, kind and wise.
He was kind and wise. Indeed, all who wrote
knew his name, yet only the few friends
of his region knew the mute misery
of his table. Frankly, I thought his poems
dull. He seemed like an old world cabinet-
maker, persisting stubbornly in meticulous
craft—patiently squaring and leveling
by eye, desperately deaf to the roaring silence
of his cobwebbed shop. He did one thing
I particularly liked. He put out peanutbutter
crackers on a plate for the mice that lived
about his writing shed. They scampered freely
everywhere, leaving their droppings in his
books and work. I would have tried to pet
their soft, white bellies, but he just watched.
His red, cragged face cupped in his red hand,
one eye glittered behind splayed fingers with
melancholic reprieve. The other, severe and weary
under the great thatch of eyebrow stared
for hours at his little mice. In late Fall
a neighbor roofing this man's house fell
from that roof and broke his neck. The poet
found him twisted grotesquely in the gray
flowerbed, mouth agape and eyes staring.
If it had been me I would have babbled
manicly of nothing else for weeks until

my wife gagged me with a look and phrase.
But he said nothing, though the storm clouds
grew. Then one night over a meal of many
drinks he began to speak, and the things
he said were terrible. To you they will seem
mad, perhaps the banal clatter of our times,
but this man could think and talk—far too well
I think. He said it was his fault the man
was dead because he gave him a beer, but
that did not matter. He said he did not care
for any of our lives or deaths, we did not
matter. He wished Dante's hell was real,
but it was not and he hated our souls
which were not real. He wished everyone
was dead, except maybe Richard Nixon,
because we were boring and deserved to die.
He was one of my fathers and he said these
things to me. Now, living day by day
to keep sober, I put down my pencil
in the dead of night and cannot sleep.
Wired with coffee, my mind buzzing
with echoes I think of him, and of Hemingway's
story about the insomniac who thought
too well. The very first opiate of the people
is opium. I had lost sight of that simple truth
and so had my beloved teacher. Oh, don't be
smug, there are still circles in our modern
diagram of hell and a spot where each can wail.
Avarice, malice, cowardice—cruel, medieval
words that hiss too strong for our enfeebled
"solipsism" or "sick psyche." Insidious whispers
of authority so safely abstract we can accept
them eagerly. I do not want my sleeping wife
and children to die, but it will come to pass.

I need not die with a stinking liver, raving
in their faces. We will submit in dignity
with generous grief. Christ! In my mind's eye
I see those mice skittering back
night after night to the dusty plate.

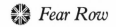 *Fear Row*

First we marched only in dark and whispers,
then muttered echoless in trenches
oozing our brothers, those stinking sleepers

who were once green and scared wayfarers.
For them too it was cheers and wenches
before they marched only in dark and whispers.

Like ghosts afraid of day, shadowless creepers,
we accepted slime, rejected human touches,
and oozed freely with our stinky, sleeping brothers.

Now, that morning still, or again propped near
any bugle, or when a party-fool mentions
war, marching in first dark and whispers

should I remember a snow of tattered papers?
A fast amazing light, one word, one wrench
of pain and we walked in dark and whispers.

Who dives for the floor anymore at firecracker
time? See those "problems" on hospital benches,
stinking sleepers who ooze with whispers
as if their dark march could make us brothers.

 *The Orphan Maker*
for David Ray

In the midst of my life
I find myself in a dark wood
where I leave the children,
carefully collecting the trail
of crumbs, their sweet cries
growing dimmer in the gathering
night. And no shade will come
to lead me back to my little ones,
or even to aching contrition.

A new child grows in my side,
conceived in innocence and reckless
joy, it now swells and mutters
like an angry dwarf. Like a money-
belt of pain, a shameful brown
paper bag hidden in a banker's coat.

Dereglement des tous les sens
they say, "nobility of the mind."
No lyric flights can assuage
the inconsolable grief of children.
All my words lose heart;
Self-loathers have no right
to love and never do.
I must forgive your love, your
suffering, and hungerless eat
the bitter gruel that I've hoarded
from you, my lonely orphans.

In the deep woods a witch waits
in her quaint house of horrors.
She is your new cruel mother
children. Obey her and love her
for she is all the world's safety.
Goodbye, I will not come or write.

✳ *Macaroni*

A Chinese noodle Polo brought home
with some queer tales and not much cash
to speak of. Now it's what I name
the feather in my cap and Doodle,
Wisenheimer, is my moniker
in New York Dutch. My pony struts
main street, farm-fed and sassy,
owned outright, envy of every slicker.
O.K. (that's American for "only kidding,"
pal), call me Hayseed if you will,
but I ain't afraid of bathwater like
you lobsters rubbing scent on your
armpit's sweat so bees buzz-bomb
you on parade. Your wives back home
are bouncing on some yokel's knee,
I'll bet. My unpowdered hair is real,
the hat is coon with a single quill
of native gamebird. Sleek and solid,
my feather jabs heavenward when
my mount highsteps it up in April mud,
unlike your fishlure plume that bobs
at every fancy syllable and giggle.
My get-up's helped unite some bloomer
strings in town, but I'm not too proud
to bow my head over the smoking beans.
Oh yeah, with a wooden spoon I'm handy,
don't need a little silver hayrake
for my vittles. I won't eat no food
that slithers. That, friend, is no baloney.

❋ L'Art Pour L'Art

Whined Gauthier. Nobody understands us
anymore, ever since we told the dummies
to mind their own business, Art is too fine
for them, they should disregard our nervous
occupations. Alas, that was not to say
they should petulantly snap their checkbooks
shut and hang their walls with poster prints.
Once we swung on great heather-scented cloaks
and floppy hats, grabbed stout walking sticks,
whistled for our dogs and set out for solace
in the countryside. No more of that will do.
Colors are all wrong out there and the behavior
of wildlife disturbs us in its mean similarity
to the insensitivity of men. For one thing,
animals are always eating each other, even
the dead. We thrill with disgust, shudder
in anticipation at the possibility for metaphor.
Yes, we are captives on this earth, fallen
weary with the world and the fictions
of other men. Only my own dreams are real,
and since they slip from memory at waking,
I make them up. *L'Art, c'est moi.* I sought
in the depths of myself a field of vicious
flowers, black velvet poppies perhaps, or a
corpse with sunset hues. But nothing was there,
and so I say truth is tedium.
Beauty does not interest us. Our great idea,
that all we see connects because we see it,
has form because we say it. Philistines malign
the sage simplicity of our forms, so we
drink up our grant money in thankless solitude,
daily dreaming the universe anew.

✳ Brancusi vs. The United States

Why is the color of my Padmaster Legal Pad
called canary? After all, the other colors
of other Padmaster Legal Pads are simply green
and white—not leaves and snow, or more
appropriately green mamba and albino rat.
Let us cherish this spark of commercial whimsy.

Certainly other legal questions have more pizzazz.
For example, "Ms. Jones, could you positively
identify the exposed organ as a penis"? Or,
"Can non-functional plumbing be objets-d'art?"
Lucky Brancusi! *Bird in Space* on display
for weeks in the crowded courtroom, daily
news stories on an artist's plight, The Famous
suddenly fast friends in arms, to be hailed
(best of all possible terms) as MODERN
in 1926 when modern really meant modern
and to have it written in law the sculpture
is "pleasing to look at and highly ornamental."
Oh, if only I could still be sued for saying
penis in a poem! But you must believe

this is a real poem, just as much as if
it is written on a real bird. My slant
rhymes are too subtle for you, my meter
pops to the regular death of cells, inaudible
to the untrained. If you really understood,
had faith in, yourselves you would be delighted
and write like this too. But Brancusi,
now a silver form glowing in some distant space,
will in light years read my work and say
(in Rumanian) "Finally, good poetry from America!"

We construct a world within
our world. Next to Africa
is India, sometimes caged
together with our indigenous
birds who come and go
as if freedom were a task.

How curious is the cruelty
of our curiosity. On TV
we watch scientists suited
up for the bush dart drugs
into fleeing beasts and staple
numbers in furry ears. All
creatures must be counted
or vanishing species will vanish.
Dog food and life insurance
are mellow patrons of wilderness.
We ourselves are scientists,
with kids in tow and peanuts, pacing
the "outer darkness" of our zoo.

Pace and sleep, sleep and pace:
out of reach the animals pad the lines
of their square kingdoms.
Squinting and pressed against rails
we read their names and countries
and thereby know them.
They smell. They are not us.
Belonging to all of us they belong
to none of us, though certainly
we have saved them from themselves.

✿ *Escape from Angola Prison*

White moonlight full on his pallid chest,
heaving wet in his open denim shirt,
so years of cigarettes whistle from his
dry throat; he pauses white-eyed,
moonfaced on the highest Tunica hill.

Below, the hounds bay, threading
bramble and thicket and behind the dogs
come men with shotguns. He knows
their faces like family: axehead sharp,
tobacco brown and country mean.

And on the flats beyond sits Angola,
as still in iron light as the model fort
in the townhall lobby, so long ago.
And there beyond is the river with another
moon wobbling in it like quicksilver.

Before him to the south, is the pulsing glow
of Baton Rouge, where infernal fire and smoke
writhe to nothing in a starless night.
It started there and will end here. Calm now,
he awaits his angel in the cool of his sweat.

And it comes chattering and chuckling out
of that southern night, bearing its own stars
and relentless beams whose pitiless sweep will
burn all shadows back. Ah, let it come.
You could not relight the lanterns in his eyes.

After an Evening of Robert Bly Slickering College Students I Think About Ornithology and How Boring I've Become

"The owl of Minerva flies only
when the shades of dusk have fallen."

Alas, the owl is not as wise
as she looks. She flies at twilight
because that light is right for all creatures
who touch her life, and for her eyes.
Yes, these grasping facts are so boring
next to the magic riddle in the poem.
Writing at my window on a morning
the color of lead, dismal with slow, persistent
rain, I like to think the doves have come
to mourn the great evil which has befallen me.
O the truth is terrible! It was no Evil
that slew my spirit, but a tedious drift
of lazy errors, petty angers, and baseless fears.
The doves are here for seeds which blackbirds
loosed from bushes in their daybreak scramble.

I love these rainy mornings for writing;
all the green world glows in easy, patient grace.
Perhaps the doves coo to say our fat,
meatheaded housecat will not go hunting
on such a day and they are free to gorge.
I do not need to understand the doves,
their throaty cries are soothing
as a mother's love, and that is all I need
to know. But the truth I do know
came from the whirl outside myself,
and from thoughts that surfaced and swept
back away—all feelings came as gifts.
I did not need to shoot a songbird twice
to know I could not afford the loss.
I think Hegel, who spoke of Minerva's bird,
meant pure wisdom comes when the day

is spent. In full sun we do not see well.
All metaphors are dubious.

I wonder if in twenty years I will awake
each morning like Robert Bly: in amazed
love with my own emotions, disgusted
by the stupidity of all other men? Ah,
he is a marvelous man, prancing like Red
Skelton (who also hates Picasso) do-
ing a parody of Balinese dance before
the trusting beards and braids roped
about his shoeless feet. It is true,
he has read more Milton than these squirming
profs who will comb the stacks, searching
for Kabir to rewin their students' love.
Let me confess I tire of my apprenticeship
of solitude and would stride forth
into the worldly places armed with music,
my third eye blazing over a flaming scarf.

In grandmother's lacquer box where I imagine
smells of Christmas orange, exotic persimmon,
I found among girlish baubles scraps of calico.
Or perhaps it was a scent of lavender and cloves,
some fancy soap, sticks of cinnamon. No papist
jewelry in her home; the box held unfinished bits
of tatting, embroidered hearts rich with simple
sentiment, faded ribbons and tinted cards depict-
ing modest virtue, still stiff from Sunday school.

So, those scraps of cloth seemed out of place,
purposeless to me until, pulled separate, I saw
logic in their geometry, a Chinese puzzle
hand-cut to while away the sabbath afternoons,
or gaslit winter evenings in Mason, Michigan
on the farm. I suppose such frivolity was
approved, since hands were busy and wits
sharpened by such play. Dark thoughts were
known to shade sweet, female minds in wintertime.

And her wits *were* sharp until those final years,
and what dark ideas deepen from that time.
Such death is cruel obscenity: all wholesome sense
tangled in infinite variety, so each harmonious
memory mocks another. Everyone she loved became
a shape and she could not match the names
with forms. Nor could slow-spinning visions
will themselves to fit in a comforting design
of time. Our creed forbids this slackness of soul.

For me it fits. My favored grandchild status
came from the whimsical accident of my middle name,
an ideal not a fact. There is still a particular texture
to these scraps and a brilliance in the calico.
Through the years I know her feeling in my living hand.

✳ *Love Letter*

Hunched close to rich humus I watched
the most mellow light from your window
square the most emerald grass in Christendom;
waiting for you, always punctual, to slip
down to my arms where I could not crush
your smell of soap and sea tight enough
to ease that wild ache. And we walked
away the night, into the good night secret
and safe, away from your father's white house
which would not presume to be different
from all the other houses, away from your
father whose nape hairs were always sharp
from the barber, who feared the dark
because I was out in it. And he was right
because we laughed (the memory of your
bell-tone laugh thrills me) at him before
and after we did what he feared most
we would do, every time. Always, after,
breathing into your breath I wished
to thank you, but I was too young
to say it right. Instead we did not stop
working our way into the earth like
thirsty roots. Yes, we were in Eden
and thorough in the rhythm of stars
rolling their turns from where we lay.
Later we too learned our sensual night
could tick and rustle with sinister
fecundity, our lover's moon shine
sullen gray on guilt and jealousy.
All is gone but your still-new sparkle
in my mind. Night sky remains
and these words, lover, go to that vast
ether. Finally to you like a prayer.

✳ *Two Friends*

after Cesare Pavese (trans. W. Arrowsmith)

I'm in the real world of men now
but I can still dream. I dream my friend
asleep on the other side of the city, too drunk
to dream. We walk up the levee, to stand
in the moon above the brown river and blue fields,
to drink. The liquor is clear like water, which
is not white you know, but tastes like the fire
in the dump. We don't wipe the jar rim because
the booze will kill anything we've got. Nor do
we talk much, nothing to say, though sometimes
one of us will begin a song. He is a fine fellow,
this friend, our blood has the same sharp taste.

My friend works when he can, not much, and I
am always busy. All we make anymore is money
and not much of that. One by one stars sprout
and bloom, throbbing in the great velvet dome.
I feel the eyes of men all around us, cold as new
silver dimes. Only the dead are friendly
in their indifferent silence. It is not real,
this dream/drunk; my friend is truly drunk far away
and I am not. To tell the truth, we are both
a little tired. The river, stars, wind and grass
just keep going on and on, over and over forever.

Tomorrow my friend's eyes will throb like stars,
his tongue will taste like spoiled sausage and I
won't feel like anything. Our women will talk
about us on the telephone and eyes will follow
our feet. People will sniff us. Sometimes the earth
is surprised by our step and wobbles, other times
it stays firm. Each morning we bring water in our hands
to our faces, and it is all then we can do.

✳ *Hazelden, 1979*

Ah Minnesota, where I trudged another hiker's
swerving path around the frozen lake under
great pines: those white-browed elders.

There the bundled poets doze and bask
by their spitting fires, nestled in warm furs
of nordic dogs and dream the wisdom of Tao.

It was there I dried my brain in an austere
season and learned from the stiffened earth
humility while time refreshed my spongy liver.

Let the fat flakes smother the ache of wrongs;
I like to think they are quiet blessings of the dead,
pure gifts of charity from beyond our human mercy.

The urge remains. I would alter a world in my
yeasty mind so my soul could fling itself
into all fantastic forms, both seen and spirit.

But what do ancient pines in winter know?
To bend to a season's pleasure. Knowing all yet
nothing they submit to the sober light.

That is the Way.